THE LITTLEST PUMPKIN

Written and Illustrated by Ember Hennig

This book is dedicated to all those who have overcome an obstacle placed in their path and who showed resilience and growth in the face of uncertainty.

Paperback ISBN: 978-1-990336-55-3
Hardcover ISBN: 978-1-990336-56-0
Contact the publisher for Library and Archives Canada catalogue information.

ALANNA RUSNAK PUBLISHING
Alanna Rusnak Publishing is an imprint of Chicken House Press
chickenhousepress.ca

The littlest pumpkin was
the smallest in the patch.

He was unlike the others
whose sizes were unmatched.

He was short and round,
and really quite cute.

But the little
pumpkin felt out of
the loop.

Day after day
the farmer came by,
watering the patch beneath
the fresh morning sky.

THE PUMPKIN PATCH

HOORAY!
IS IT TODAY ?
YES IT IS!

All throughout the field
there was chitter and chatter,
the pumpkins had been raising
up quite a clatter.

The news was out:
Pumpkin Picking Day!
and with that, all the pumpkins
shouted, "Hooray!"

The littlest pumpkin
still did not know...
what pumpkin picking day was,
and where he might go.

WELCOME

Pumpkin Picking Day
was the day of the year,
that all of the patch
would shout and cheer.

The farmer drove down the driveway
and swung open the gate,
ensuring the day
did not start too late.

The day has begun,
the crowd is here,
and the littlest pumpkin
has nothing to fear.

Though he still did not know
where he would go,
the pumpkin's face
began to glow.

WELCOME

The crowd of people
rushed into the patch,
each person choosing
a pumpkin to snatch.

The littlest pumpkin
waited all day,
for someone to pick him
and take him away.

"PERFECT" PUMPKIN
WEIGHT
SCALE

As the day drew on
his face grew long.
No one had picked him.
What was so wrong?

Was he too little?
Was he too small?
The pumpkin didn't think
that was a good reason at all.

All the other pumpkins
had gone away,
but no one picked the littlest
pumpkin today.

The littlest pumpkin
was all alone,
as the weeks flew by,
and the weeds had grown.

The leaves had fallen,
the trees had gone bare,
and the littlest pumpkin
felt a chill in the air.

Winter would soon
be on its way,
the littlest pumpkin
wondered if he'd be okay.

One cold morning, the farmer
walked through the fields
to check on the harvest
and measure the yield.

Out in the patch,
the farmer saw quite a mess,
a giant pile of leaves,
that caused him some stress.

He walked to the patch
to clean up the leaves,
and found quite a surprise
hidden underneath.

The littlest pumpkin,
though no longer small,
had grown to be
almost five feet tall.

The farmer ran back
to the barn in a flash
and the next thing you heard
was a giant crash.

Out he came,
a red wagon in tow,
to wheel the pumpkin
to the fall show.

WELCOME
TO TOWN

The farmer rolled him
all the way to town;
that made the pumpkin's frown
turn upside down.

He made it just in time
for the show to begin,
so the farmer entered him
for a chance to win.

Those who had left him all alone,
could now see the littlest pumpkin
had grown.

FALL FAIR
REGISTRATION

1ST
WINNER
JUDGES TABLE
10
10
THAT LITTLE PUMPKIN GOT SO BIG!
WOW!
HE WAS SO SMALL?

When it was time
to take the stage,
the judges and crowd
were all amazed.

The crowd had a puzzled look
on their face,
as the not-so-littlest pumpkin
took first place.

Never judge a pumpkin
by its size,
as you may be in
for quite a surprise.

The littlest pumpkin
was surprised indeed.
Remember, all pumpkins grow
from the same tiny seed.

The End